P9-CEH-242

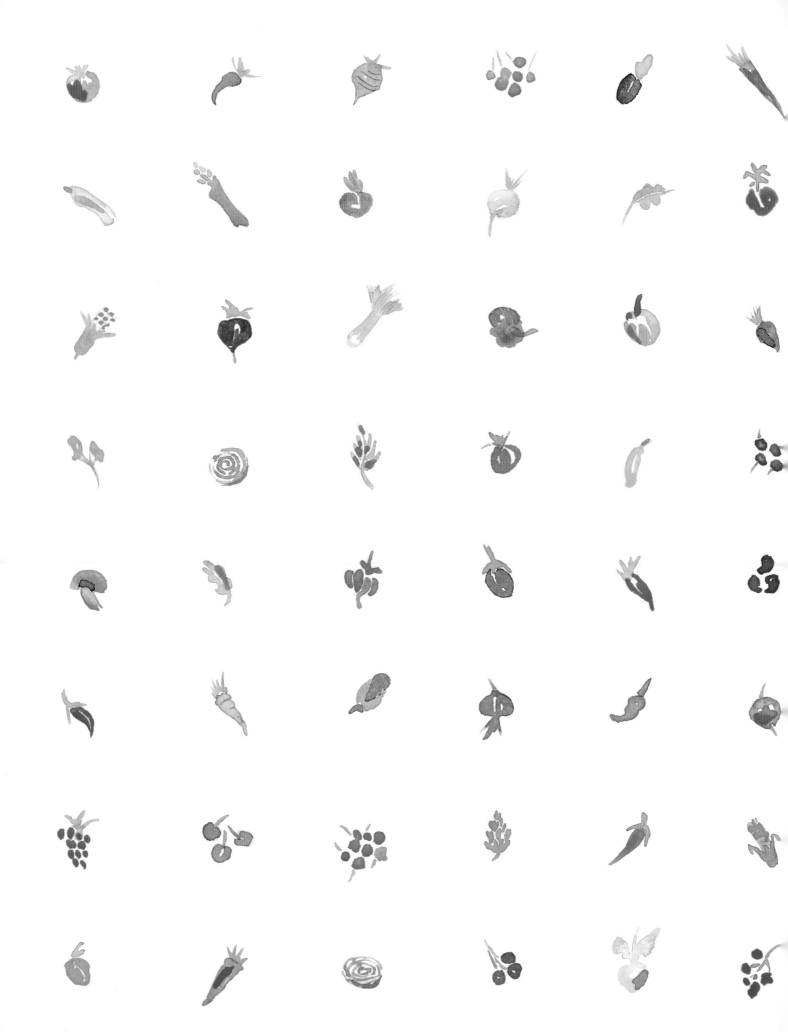

First Garden

THE WHITE HOUSE GARDEN

AND HOW IT GREW

WRITTEN AND
ILLUSTRATED BY

Robbin Gourley

FOREWORD BY ALICE WATERS

CLARION BOOKS
HOUGHTON MIFFLIN HARCOURT
BOSTON • NEW YORK • 2011

To Elouise, Betty Lou Faye Irene, and Sue—
sisters, gardeners, and cooks who hoed the row before me—R.G.

This book never would have grown without editor Marcia Leonard, who tilled, plowed,
and planted alongside me from the very beginning; vice-president and publisher Dinah Stevenson, who
harnessed the wind, water, and sun; senior designer Kerry Martin, who harvested the bounty; and publishing
heroes Elisabeth Scharlatt, Margaret Ferguson, and Frances Foster, who showed me the proper way to
do things. Ladies, there will always be a place for you at my table.

Clarion Books
215 Park Avenue South
New York, New York 10003

Clarion Books is an imprint of Houghton Mifflin Harcourt Publishing Company.
www.hmhbooks.com

The illustrations were executed in watercolor.
The text was set in 16-point Eureka.
Book design by Kerry Martin
Hand-lettering by Bernard Maisner

Library of Congress Cataloging-in-Publication Data
Gourley, Robbin.
First garden : the White House garden and how it grew / written and illustrated by Robbin Gourley.
p. cm.
ISBN 978-0-547-48224-8 (hardcover nonfiction picture book : alk. paper) 1. White House Gardens (Washington, D.C.)—
Juvenile literature. 2. Obama, Michelle, 1964– —Juvenile literature. 3. Kitchen gardens—
Washington (D.C.)—Juvenile literature. 4. Gardens—Washington (D.C.) —Juvenile literature. I. Title.

SB466.U7W483 2011
712.09753—dc22

2010024643

Manufactured in China
LEO 10 9 8 7 6 5 4 3 2 1
4500260444

FOREWORD BY ALICE WATERS

A vegetable garden on the White House grounds . . . what a beautiful symbol for America! Its creation—at our country's most visible address—is a joyful return to the values of Thomas Jefferson. It is a victory garden in the truest sense: a demonstration to the world that as Americans, we are dedicated to the stewardship of the land and the nourishment of our citizens.

Growing delicious seasonal fruits and vegetables on the White House lawn does so much more than just feed our First Family. The garden teaches us about the beauties of nature and the bounty that comes from the earth; it shows that local, affordable, healthful food should be a right for all people, not just the privilege of a few; and it energizes and inspires the nation, creating a lasting vision for generations to come.

Alice Waters

ALICE WATERS is the founder and owner of Chez Panisse Restaurant and Café in Berkeley, California. She is also the founder of the Edible Schoolyard program, which creates organic garden- and kitchen-classrooms in urban public schools. Gardens are tended and harvested by students, and hands-on ecology and nutrition lessons are woven into the curriculum.

this house and all that hereafter inhabit it.

I pray heaven to bestow the best of blessings on

THE WHITE HOUSE is the official home of the president of the United States of America. The first president, George Washington, supervised its construction beginning in 1792, but he never lived there. In fact, work *still* wasn't finished when the second president, John Adams, and his wife, Abigail, moved in eight years later.

Since then, each new president has made changes and additions to the furnishings, the building, and the grounds. The White House now has one hundred and thirty-two rooms, counting the offices in two wings. There are thirty-five bathrooms, eleven bedrooms, two kitchens, three dining rooms, one library, one bowling alley—and a movie theater.

RONALD REAGAN

The White House sits on eighteen acres of land, called the President's Park, in the heart of Washington, D.C. The park includes the Rose Garden, where the president sometimes gives speeches;

the Jacqueline Kennedy Garden, where the president often entertains informally;

and the Children's Garden, which has a goldfish pond and an apple tree that's perfect for climbing.

There's also a swimming pool, a basketball court, a tennis court, a landing pad for the president's helicopter, and a huge open area called the South Lawn—home to the annual Easter Egg Roll.

Over the years, more than fifty children have lived in the White House, and the South Lawn has been their backyard and playground.

TAD LINCOLN, son of Abraham Lincoln, kept two ponies in the White House stables.

BENJAMIN MCKEE, grandson of Benjamin Harrison, drove a cart pulled by a goat named Old Whiskers.

KERMIT ROOSEVELT, son of Theodore Roosevelt, played fetch with his terrier Jack—one of five family dogs.

JOHN KENNEDY, JR., son of
John F. Kennedy, liked to splash in
the White House fountain.

TRICIA NIXON, daughter of
Richard Nixon, was married in
the Rose Garden.

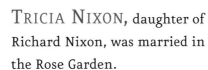

AMY CARTER, daughter of
Jimmy Carter, had slumber parties
in her tree house on the South Lawn.

When Barack Obama became the forty-fourth president, he moved into the White House with his wife, First Lady Michelle Obama, their daughters, Malia and Sasha, and Mrs. Obama's mother, Marian Robinson. Soon they added a dog named Bo to the family.

As First Lady and as a mom, Mrs. Obama was concerned about the health of the American people. She believed we should think about what we eat and where our food comes from. And she wanted her family—all families—to become healthier by eating more vegetables and fruits and by eating meals together at the table.

One day early in 2009, Mrs. Obama watched Malia and Sasha play on the South Lawn. She gazed out at the large expanse of grass—where President Taft's cow, Pauline, once grazed and where President Wilson once kept a flock of sheep—and made a decision. She would plant a kitchen garden full of fruits and vegetables, right there on the White House lawn.

The president thought it was a wonderful idea.

Other First Families have had vegetable gardens at the White House, but there hadn't been one since Eleanor Roosevelt's Victory Garden. It was planted in 1943, during World War II, to show Americans the importance of growing extra food and conserving fuel to support the war effort.

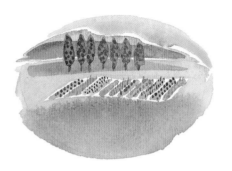

JOHN ADAMS

1800 President John Adams planned the first White House garden so that First Families could enjoy fresh fruits and vegetables.

THOMAS JEFFERSON

1801 President Thomas Jefferson added ornamental trees and fruit trees to the grounds. He also grazed cattle on the South Lawn.

JOHN QUINCY ADAMS

1825 President John Quincy Adams described the garden during his term of office as two acres covered with "forest and fruit-trees, shrubs, hedges, vegetables, kitchen and medicinal herbs, hot-house plants, flowers, and weeds."

ANDREW JACKSON

1835 President Andrew Jackson built the White House orangery, a greenhouse for year-round tropical fruit.

But after the war ended and food was more readily available at grocery stores, most Americans lost interest in backyard gardening.

Mrs. Obama began planning for the kitchen garden right away. She would need lots of help, but she knew of some very good workers.

WOODROW & EDITH WILSON

1918 President Woodrow Wilson and his wife, Edith, grazed sheep on the lawn as an "edible landscape" that trimmed the grass and provided wool and mutton.

ELEANOR ROOSEVELT

1943 First Lady Eleanor Roosevelt planted a Victory Garden on the lawn and encouraged citizens to plant their own gardens. It's estimated that by the end of World War II, twenty million homeowners had Victory Gardens and produced close to forty percent of the fresh vegetables eaten in America.

Eleanor Roosevelt (1884–1962)

PATRICIA NIXON

1973 First Lady Patricia Nixon organized spring and fall tours of the White House grounds, to share the beauty of the gardens with the American public.

Cultivators of the earth are the most valuable citizens. They are the

In March, on the first day of spring, Mrs. Obama invited twenty-three fifth-grade boys and girls from Bancroft Elementary School in Washington, D.C., to come and help her begin work on the garden. White House gardeners had marked off a 1,100-square-foot space on the lawn. Mrs. Obama showed the children how to dig up the grass and break up the earth beneath it. With the assistance of the White House kitchen staff, they turned the soil with shovels and spades and hands.

The gardeners added organic material to help the vegetables grow and keep insects away. And beekeeper Charlie Brandts installed a beehive nearby, a home for about 60,000 bees that would pollinate plants and make honey for the White House.

Seedlings were started in the White House greenhouse. Some were from seeds passed down by plants first grown two hundred years ago by Thomas Jefferson! They came from his garden in Monticello, Virginia, and were donated by the Thomas Jefferson Foundation.

In April, the children from Bancroft Elementary came back to help plant the kitchen garden. Mrs. Obama showed them how to dig a shallow hole in the soft, warm earth, plant a seedling in it, and mound and tap the soil around it for support.

On hands and knees they worked, carefully placing young shoots of Thomas Jefferson lettuces, cabbages, and spinach. They planted parsley and thyme, eggplant and cucumber, carrots, kale, and sweet potatoes,

Chard

Kale

raspberries and blueberries. In all, they planted fifty-five varieties of herbs, fruits, and vegetables.

The president said, "NO BEETS!" So it is a no-beet garden.

When they finished sowing the shoots from the seedlings, the children gave the garden a deep, gentle watering. At the end of their day's work, laid out in neat rows—ready to grow, bursting with promise—was the First Garden.

In every garden, there is ongoing work and there are problems to deal with. There are weeds. Mrs. Obama said, "Everyone will have to weed. Even the president." There are plant-destroying bugs. In the First Garden, ladybugs and praying mantises were introduced to control harmful insect populations. And nasturtiums, zinnias, and marigolds—flowers that naturally keep bugs away—were planted. There are animal pests. In the First Garden, some of the plants are covered with fine netting to keep birds, squirrels, and rabbits away.

In the First Garden, there are a few unusual problems to deal with as well. The wind created by the president's helicopter could knock over the beehive, so it had to be fastened securely to its stand and the stand set in concrete. The garden is very popular, and there are many people who want to see it. To protect it from being trampled and sampled, visitors are taken around by guides. Bo had to be kept out of the garden, because dogs like to dig.

Mrs. Obama enlisted Cristeta Comerford, the White House executive chef, and Bill Yosses, the dessert chef, to begin planning vegetable and fruit dishes for the First Family and for guests of the White House. Sam Kass, an assistant chef, was appointed food initiative coordinator to oversee the garden. It took just six weeks for the First Garden to start producing food ready for harvest.

Yummy!

Delicious!

Scrumptious!

Divine!

In June, Cristeta served a salad course made of ingredients from the garden to twenty important guests of the president. By July, Bill was making desserts with rhubarb and honey. As the garden grew, it could provide vegetable courses and salads for as many as one hundred and forty White House guests—or appetizers for as many as a thousand. It helped feed the First Family and the staff, and it provided food to Miriam's Kitchen, an organization that prepares and serves free, healthy, homemade meals to homeless men and women in Washington, D.C.

To celebrate the success of the kitchen garden, Mrs. Obama planned a harvest party for August. The invitation list included the student gardeners from Bancroft Elementary, and Sam, Cristeta, Bill, and Charlie. After being away from the garden for four months, the children were surprised at how much everything had grown and how much was ready to be eaten.

Mrs. Obama showed them how to cut the lettuces at ground level. They picked peas and berries. Then they all trooped into the White House kitchen, where Cristeta had them wash the lettuce, pick over the peas to get the good ones, and throw out the tiny rocks that can cling to vegetables fresh from the garden. With Cristeta and Sam, they prepared a salad and decorated cupcakes with raspberries and blueberries. Then they all sat down at picnic tables on the South Lawn to enjoy their feast.

Over the summer, the First Garden produced more than a thousand pounds of food, and the bees produced one hundred and thirty-four pounds of honey—roughly eleven gallons.

In September, Mrs. Obama hosted a dinner for the spouses of international leaders. It was a very elegant affair, and each guest was given a one-of-a-kind china tea set and a hand-blown glass container full of White House honey.

The First Garden was now famous around the world!

Winters in Washington, D.C., are usually fairly mild, so gardening can go on year round. In December, Sam oversaw the installation of a hoop house, a set of metal bars placed over the garden beds and covered with tight-fitting fabric. The sun warms the hoop house during the day, and the fabric traps the heat, so the plants don't freeze overnight. This means the First Family and guests of the White House can enjoy fresh spinach, lettuce, carrots, mustard greens, chard, and cabbage until it's time to prepare the soil and plant new seeds in spring.

It doesn't take a South Lawn to make a kitchen garden. It takes a windowsill and a pot, a small part of your own backyard, or a plot in a community garden.

You can follow the same steps taken by the White House:

🌱 Prepare the soil. 🥕 Plant your seeds or shoots.

🧅 Keep out weeds and pests. 🌽 Harvest.

🌿 Save seeds for next year's garden.

And whether or not you have a garden, you can make small changes for better nutrition and health. You can eat like the president's family.

 Buy more local produce.  Add more fruits and vegetables to every meal.

 Eat fewer processed and sugary foods.  Eat out less often.

 Sit down as a family for meals.

More than two hundred years ago, while building a new nation on principles of independence and self-reliance, our country's founders planted gardens to bring nourishment to their families and beauty to their surroundings. They understood that the more you garden, the more you grow.

The White House kitchen garden marks a glorious return to those early ideals. And who knows? If beets are planted there, the president may even grow to like them.

GOOD REASONS TO GARDEN

Gardens produce delicious fresh food that nourishes our bodies and keeps us healthy.

Gardens conserve energy and resources by cutting back on our need for packaged, transported, and warehoused foods.

Gardening doesn't require a lot of fancy, expensive tools. Produce from the garden costs less than store-bought produce.

Gardening is great exercise. It takes plenty of lifting, bending, and stretching to plant, weed, and harvest a garden.

Tending a garden is a good way to relieve stress. It can help create a happy mind and a peaceful spirit.

Extra food and flowers from the garden make great gifts for friends and neighbors.

Home gardening can help us appreciate the work of those who farm for a living.

Compost made from kitchen scraps, leaves, and yard clippings can be added to the garden soil. It's a way to help plants grow while recycling and reducing waste.

Gardens create beautiful landscapes for people to enjoy.

Gardens attract birds, bees, and butterflies. Trees and shrubs offer shade and shelter for wildlife.

Gardening is an activity that can be shared by people of all ages, from little kids to grandparents. It can be shared by neighborhoods, communities, and towns.

Gardeners are stewards and protectors of the land.

RECIPES FROM THE WHITE HOUSE

The following recipes were distributed by the White House at two open press events: the Healthy Kids Fair on October 21, 2009, and Chefs Move to Schools on June 4, 2010.

BAKED SLICED APPLES

6 apples, cored and sliced
½ oz. butter
½ tsp. ground cinnamon
¼ cup maple syrup, brown sugar, or honey
⅛ tsp. ground nutmeg
½ cup rolled oats
½ tsp. salt
¼ cup raisins or any dried fruit
¼ cup apple juice

Preheat oven to 350 degrees. Combine all ingredients. Place in buttered baking pan and bake for 45 minutes or until a golden brown crust appears. You may also add a cup of your favorite nuts for added protein and flavor. Serve warm with baked eggs for a nutritious balanced breakfast. Serves 8.

Baked Eggs

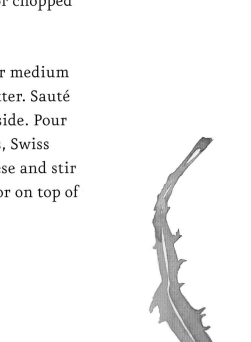

6 large eggs, beaten
salt and pepper to taste
¼ oz. butter
1 ½ tsp. vegetable oil
1 ¾ cups potatoes, diced
2 cups Swiss chard, chopped*
1 cup cooked turkey breakfast sausage, sliced, cubed, or chopped
1 cup cheddar cheese, grated

Season eggs with salt and pepper. Warm sauté pan over medium heat. (The pan should not get too hot.) Add oil and butter. Sauté potatoes and Swiss chard, remove from pan, and set aside. Pour eggs into pan to form a base. Place the cooked potatoes, Swiss chard, and sausage on top. Distribute evenly. Add cheese and stir once. Eggs can be finished in a low (300-degree) oven or on top of the stove. Cook until firm but not dry. Serves 8.

*Any vegetable may be substituted.

Zucchini Quesadillas

1 Tbs. canola oil
1 medium zucchini, diced small
1 small onion, finely chopped
½ tsp. cumin
½ tsp. chili powder
½ tsp. dried parsley (optional)
1 ½ cups shredded reduced-fat cheddar cheese
6 8-inch flour or corn tortillas
½ cup mild salsa
1 15-oz. can beans (white or lima)

Preheat oven to 400 degrees. Lightly oil a nonstick baking sheet and set aside. Heat oil in nonstick pan. Add zucchini, onion, cumin, chili powder, parsley, and half of the cheese and cook until cheese is melted.

To assemble quesadillas, spread the filling on a tortilla and top with salsa and beans. Place another tortilla on top. Place on baking sheet and sprinkle with remaining cheese. Bake until tortillas are crisp and cheese is melted. Cut into quarters and serve warm.

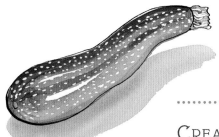

Creamy Salsa Dip

1 jar salsa, approximately 1 cup
⅓ cup cream cheese, room temperature
tortilla chips or cut vegetables

Mix salsa and cream cheese together and serve with chips or vegetables.

Sweet & Zesty Popcorn

1 bag microwaveable popcorn, preferably low-fat
½ cup pretzel sticks
½ cup raisins
½ cup shelled roasted peanuts
2 Tbs. brown sugar
⅓ cup Parmesan cheese

Place popcorn in microwave and cook as per instructions on bag. Place cooked popcorn in a large bowl. Add the other ingredients and gently mix, trying not to break the pretzel sticks. Popcorn will keep for two days if placed in an airtight container and kept at room temperature.

Vegetable Dip

1 Tbs. fresh lemon juice
½ cup extra virgin olive oil
1 tsp. garlic, minced
1 tsp. kosher salt
2 cups Greek yogurt
1 cup cucumber, peeled, seeded, and diced
½ cup onion, finely diced

Add lemon juice, olive oil, garlic, and salt to yogurt. Add cucumber and onion and mix well. Chill for at least one hour. Serve with an assortment of cut vegetables.

Grilled Chicken Salad with Herb Sherry Vinaigrette

Ingredients for salad:
6 chicken breasts, 6 oz. each
1 Tbs. fresh thyme, chopped
zest of 1 lemon
6 sprigs chives, chopped
2 lbs. of assorted garden greens, arugula, and baby spinach

Marinate chicken with herbs, lemon zest, and olive oil. Season with salt and pepper, and grill. When cool, cut into bite-sized pieces. Wash lettuce, tear it into pieces, and place it in a large bowl. To assemble salad, add grilled chicken and vinaigrette (recipe follows) and toss until salad leaves are coated. Serve immediately. Serves 6.

Ingredients for vinaigrette:
¼ cup sherry vinegar
juice of 2 lemons
1 shallot, finely minced
1 Tbs. fresh oregano, chopped
1 Tbs. fresh basil, chopped
2 Tbs. honey
Salt and pepper to taste
1 cup extra virgin olive oil

Place all ingredients, except olive oil, in a bowl. Slowly whisk olive oil into mixture until emulsified.

RHUBARB STRAWBERRY CRISP

Ingredients for crisp topping:
8 oz. cold butter
2 ¼ cups flour
¾ cup light brown sugar
½ cup sugar
½ cup quick cooking oats

Directions for crisp topping:
Cut butter into small pieces. Place butter, flour, light brown sugar, sugar, and oats in food processor and pulse briefly. Set aside.

Ingredients for filling:
2 lbs. rhubarb stalks, chopped
juice of 1 lemon
⅓ cup sugar
½ tsp. cinnamon
Pinch salt
3 Tbs. cornstarch
¼ tsp. ground cardamom
1 lb. strawberries

Directions for filling:
Preheat oven to 350 degrees. In a large bowl, toss rhubarb with lemon juice, sugar, cinnamon, salt, cornstarch, and cardamom. Hull strawberries, cut in half, and toss together with the rhubarb mixture. Transfer to baking dish and cover with crisp topping about ¾ inch thick. Bake for 50 minutes or until topping is browned and fruit is bubbling.

RESOURCES

Books About U.S. Presidents, the White House—and Bo

Bausum, Ann. *Our Country's Presidents: All You Need to Know About the Presidents, from George Washington to Barack Obama.* Washington, D.C.: National Geographic Children's Books, 2009.

Grace, Catherine O'Neill, in cooperation with the White House Historical Association. *The White House: An Illustrated History.* New York: Scholastic, 2003.

O'Connor, Jane. *If the Walls Could Talk: Family Life at the White House.* Illustrated by Gary Hovland. New York: Simon & Schuster/Paula Wiseman Books, 2004.

Our White House: Looking In, Looking Out. Various authors and illustrators in cooperation with the National Children's Book Literacy Alliance. Cambridge, Mass.: Candlewick Press, 2008.

Rinaldo, Denise. *White House Q & A.* New York: HarperCollins Publishers, 2007.

Staake, Bob. *The First Pup: The Real Story of How Bo Got to the White House.* New York: Feiwel & Friends, 2010.

Websites About the White House

www.presidentialpetmuseum.com/whitehousepets-1.htm. Photos and information about presidents and their pets.

www.time.com/time/photogallery/0,29307,1869753_1821295,00.html. From *Time* magazine, a photo album of presidents and their children.

upstairsatthewhitehouse.com/children_of_presidents.html. The historian Doug Wead tracks the lives of the parents, siblings, and children of U.S. presidents.

www.whitehouse.gov. All things about the White House and the U.S. government, including its policies, issues, legislation, and administration, and the current presidency.

www.whitehousehistory.org/index.html. The White House Historical Association website, dedicated to enhancing the understanding, appreciation, and enjoyment of the White House.

www.whitehousemuseum.org/index.htm. An unofficial virtual museum of the White House.

Books About Gardens and Gardening for Young Readers

Brown, Peter. *The Curious Garden*. New York: Little, Brown & Company, 2009.

Cole, Henry. *Jack's Garden*. New York: Greenwillow Books, 1995.

Gardening with Children. Various authors. Illustrated by Sam Tomasello. New York: Brooklyn Botanic Garden, 2007.

Grow It, Cook It: Simple Gardening Projects and Delicious Recipes. New York: DK Publishing, 2008.

Krezel, Cindy. *101 Kid-Friendly Plants: Fun Plants and Family Garden Projects*. West Chicago, Ill.: Ball Publishing, 2008.

Lin, Grace. *The Ugly Vegetables*. Watertown, Mass.: Charlesbridge Publishing, 2009.

Lovejoy, Sharon. *Roots, Shoots, Buckets and Boots: Gardening Together with Children*. New York: Workman Publishing Company, 1999.

Ready Set Grow. New York: DK Publishing, 2010.

Siddals, Mary McKenna. *Compost Stew: An A to Z Recipe for the Earth*. Illustrated by Ashley Wolff. Berkeley, Calif.: Tricycle Press, 2010.

Waters, Alice, with Daniel Duane. *Edible Schoolyard: A Universal Idea*. Photos by David Liittschwager. San Francisco: Chronicle Books, 2008

Websites About Gardening

www.greeneducationfoundation.org. A website focusing on children and education, with the goal of fostering the next generation of environmental stewards.

www.kidsgardening.org. A website promoting home, school, and community gardening as a means of connecting people, plants, and the environment.

www.kitchengardeners.org. Information provided by a community of 20,000 kitchen gardeners from more than one hundred countries.

www.obamafoodorama.blogspot.com. An independent blog about the White House, the Obama food initiative, and food politics.

www.plantingseedsblog.com. A gardening blog that supplies information about planting, growing, harvesting, cooking, and gardening folklore and superstition.

Websites Supporting Local Agriculture

www.communitygarden.org. A website supporting community greening in urban and rural communities, with links to locate your nearest community garden.

www.csrees.usda.gov/Extension. Links to nationwide cooperative extension system offices that can provide agriculture and gardening information to people in communities of all sizes.

www.localharvest.org. A website to locate farmers' markets, family farms, and other sources of sustainably grown food across the United States.

....

Your local botanical garden, gardening club, YMCA, or arboretum may offer gardening workshops, classes, and information.

Many newspapers have a dining section that provides recipes and information on cooking and carries reports on farmers' markets and local food initiatives.

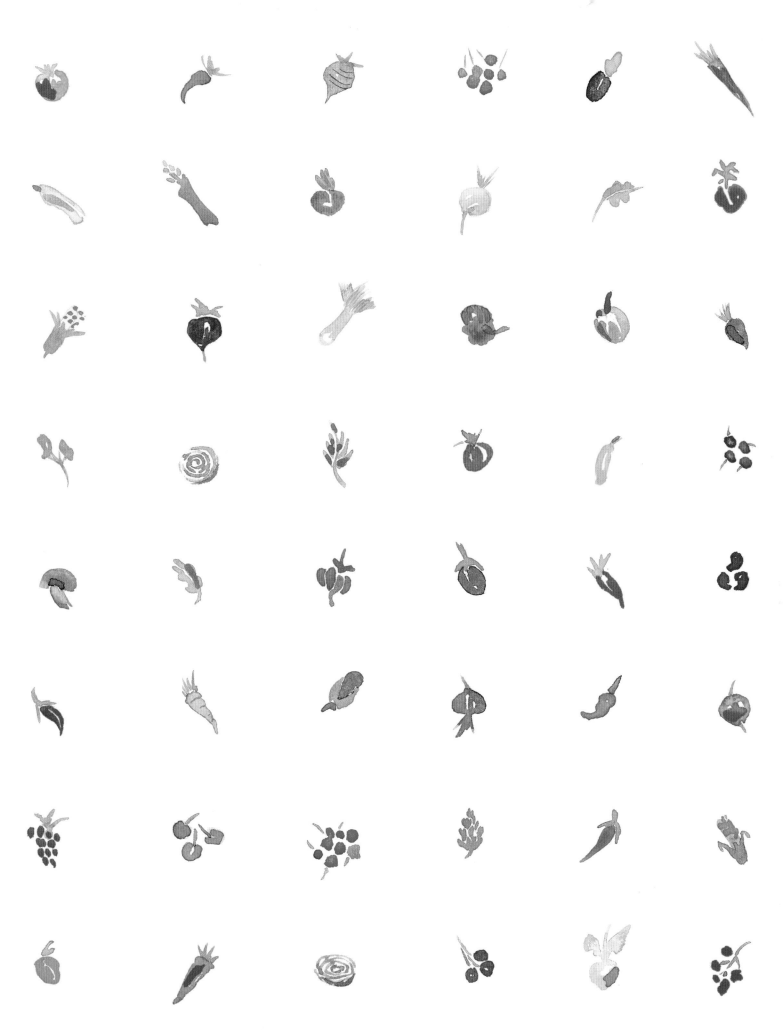

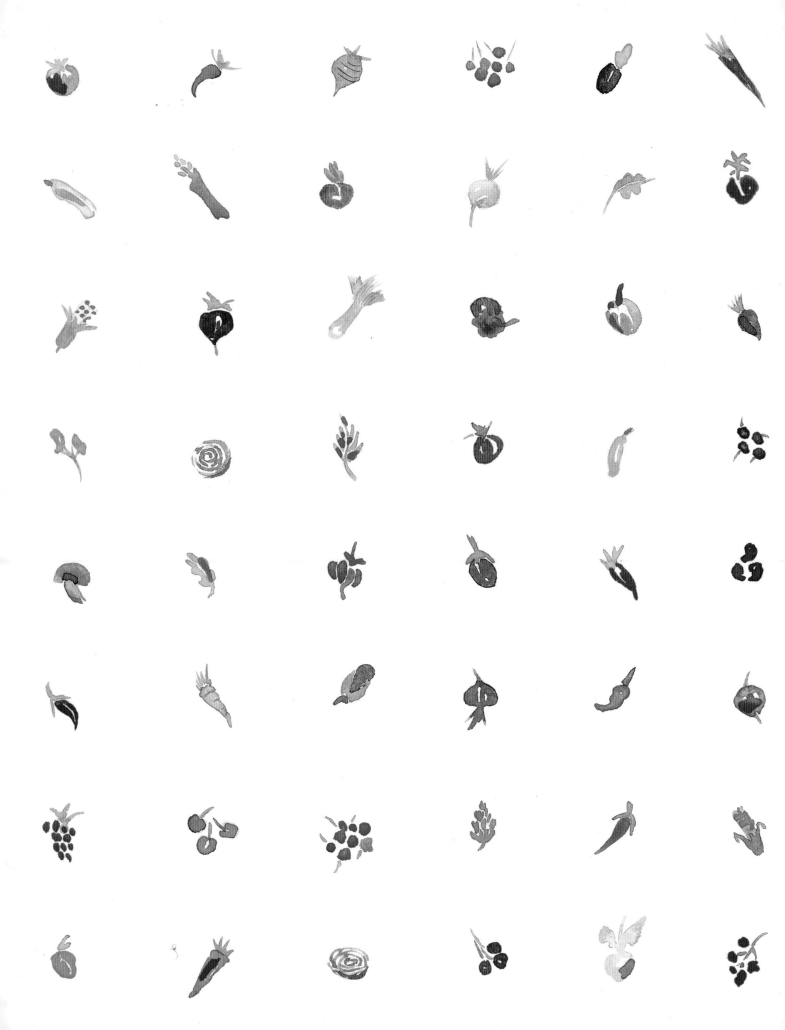